CURVES, SLIDERS, AND SINKERS

PITCH LIKE A PRO WITH A WIFFLE® BALL

by Jason Sutherland

Random House New York

To Mary K., for whom I'll always be up to bat.
Many thanks to Mark Odegard, Izzy Lefebvre, Bill Sutherland,
and the rest of the Boyz in the Three-Five.

Copyright ©1996 by becker&mayer!, Ltd. All rights reserved under International and Pan-American Copyright Conventions. Published in the United States by Random House, Inc., New York, and simultaneously in Canada by Random House of Canada Limited, Toronto.

ISBN: 0-679-88081 X
Printed in Canada 10 9 8 7 6 5 4 3 2 1
Wiffle® is a registered trademark owned by
the Wiffle Ball, Inc., Shelton, CT 06484.

Illustrations by Sylvia Shapiro
Wiffle® Ball Photo by Jason Sutherland
Interior Design by Leandra Jones

Notice to Parents and Coaches

All of the pitches described in this book are safe to throw with the included Wiffle® ball! Although throwing some of these pitches with a regular baseball could be damaging to the arms of pitchers under the age of fourteen, the Wiffle® ball is specially designed to eliminate the risk of injury.

Contents

Introduction 5
Why Do Balls Curve? 6
The Windup 8
The Curveball 12
The Fastball 14
The Screwball 16
The Slider 18
The Knuckleball 20
The Change-up 22
The Sinker 24
The Riser 26
Pitching Tips 28
Home Run Derby 30

Introduction

It takes more than just a strong arm to be a pitcher in major league baseball. It takes a blend of strength, talent, strategy, and courage. This book will introduce you to the basics of pitching and teach you how to throw everything from a fastball to a screwball. Although breaking pitches—pitches in which the ball curves, sinks, or rises—are thrown by major and minor league pitchers, developing players shouldn't throw these pitches with a regular baseball because of the potential for injury to their arms. Even Frank Viola, a master of the curveball, didn't try to throw a curve until he was a junior in high school. But with the Wiffle® ball, breaking pitches can be thrown—and mastered—without fear of injury.

This book will teach you baseball's most important pitches and provide you with rules for a game you can play so you can practice the pitches with your friends. Grab the Wiffle® ball and follow along with the diagrams!

Why Do Balls Curve?

Before we get into the pitches, it's a good idea to understand the way things work. A breaking pitch's magic begins when the ball leaves your hand. The ball travels toward the plate with different amounts of spin, depending on how it was pitched. As the ball moves through the air, the spinning displaces air on both sides of the ball.

If a ball is spinning counterclockwise when viewed from overhead, it releases the air on the left side later than the air on the right side. This produces a little jet of air streaming to the right, which pushes the ball to the left. This is called the Magnus effect, which is named after Gustav Magnus, the scientist who discovered it. If the ball spins faster, the Magnus force is greater, and the curve of the ball's flight is bigger. If the ball has a rougher surface, it can hold on to the air longer, once again creating a larger Magnus force and a larger curve on the ball. This is why pitchers sometimes scuff the baseball to throw a better curveball, even though it's against the rules.

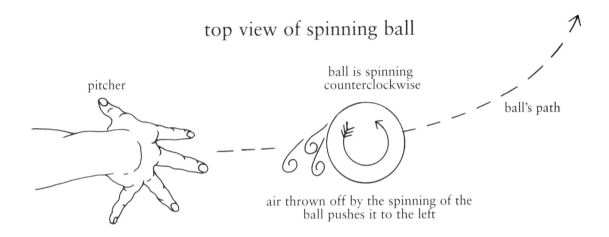

Pitchers who use a regular baseball to throw breaking pitches make the ball spin by adjusting their throw as the ball leaves their hand. This is stressful on your arm and can cause muscle damage if not done properly. With the Wiffle® ball, the slots on the ball make it spin. All you have to do is make certain the slots are facing the right direction, wind up, and throw!

The Windup

In order to pitch accurately, you must develop a smooth pitching motion and stick to it for every delivery. The most important things to remember when pitching are to hold the ball correctly for a specific pitch and to use the same motion for every pitch. With practice, you'll develop a natural feel for throwing the ball exactly where you want. When you have a smooth pitching motion, you'll be able to throw many different types of pitches just by changing the way you hold the ball.

A Note for Left-Handed Pitchers: *If you throw left-handed, hold the illustrations up to a mirror. The way the illustrations appear in the mirror is how you should hold the Wiffle® ball in your left hand. Remember, the ball will curve in the opposite direction of a ball thrown by a right-hander.*

The pitching motion can be divided into the following six steps:

1. Face the batter with the ball hidden behind your body. Decide what type of pitch you want to throw and be certain to grip the ball properly. Don't let the batter see the grip you have on the ball or you'll give away the type of pitch you're going to throw.

2. Swing your arms up and over your head, keeping the ball hidden with your other hand.

3 Pull back your throwing arm and lift your opposite leg at the same time.

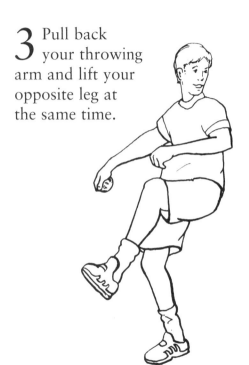

4 Take a step toward the plate, bringing your throwing arm straight up and over your head.

5 Continue to bring your arm forward over your head and release the ball with a slight flick of the wrist; this can be accomplished by keeping your wrist fairly loose as you throw.

6 Follow through and be ready to field a hit ball. As soon as you've released the ball, your role switches from pitcher to fielder.

The Curveball

Perhaps the oldest breaking pitch in baseball is the curveball. A curveball is a pitch that curves to the left when thrown by a right-handed pitcher. The curveball is credited to William Arthur "Candy" Cummings, who refined the curving pitch by throwing clamshells on the beach. Much to the relief of clams everywhere, Candy was able to apply what he learned to baseball by twisting his wrist and holding on to the ball slightly longer than when he threw a fastball. Fortunately for you, you don't have to throw clamshells or twist your wrist to throw a curveball—the Wiffle® ball is specially designed for throwing curves.

To throw a curveball, hold the ball in your right hand as shown in the illustration, with the slots of the ball facing to your left. Your first two fingers and your thumb should be placed along the seam that divides the two halves of the ball. Use a standard pitching motion to deliver the ball. The ball should curve to the left side of the plate. If you are pitching left-handed, reverse the grip for your left hand. The ball will curve to the right of the plate.

Perhaps the best curveball in baseball's history was thrown by a man who was missing two of his fingers! Mordecai "Three Finger" Brown played fourteen seasons, throwing one of baseball's finest curves with a hand that had been badly damaged in a farming accident. Brown credited his unique configuration of fingers for his incredible curveball.

The Fastball

The fastball is every professional pitcher's basic pitch. A pitcher without a fastball is like a batter without a good swing. Besides speed, the most important skill for throwing a fastball is the ability to control where the ball goes.

To throw a fastball, hold the Wiffle® ball between your thumb and the first two fingers of your hand, with the slots facing toward your palm. The smooth side of the ball should be facing out. Use a smooth overhead windup and pitch, and you've got the fastball. The ball should fly straight and fast to the plate.

One pitcher with a legendary fastball was Nolan Ryan, who in 1974 threw a pitch that was clocked at 100.8 miles per hour! The incredible speed with which he could throw the ball helped make him one of the best pitchers in baseball.

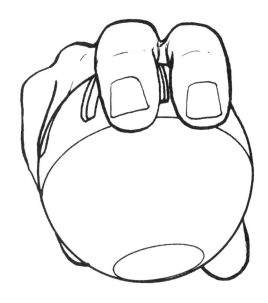

Although speed isn't everything in baseball, it still plays an important role in delivering a great pitch. Just ask Randy "The Big Unit" Johnson of the Seattle Mariners. Johnson's blazing fastball helped take his team to the 1995 American League Championship Series against the Cleveland Indians. One of Johnson's fastballs during the championship was clocked at 98 miles per hour!

The Screwball

A pitch that flies like a curveball but curves in the other direction is called a screwball. To throw this pitch, hold the Wiffle® ball in your pitching hand between your thumb and your first and second fingers. Rotate the ball so your grip fingers are along the middle seam and the slots are on the side of your third and fourth fingers.

Throw the screwball with a standard overhead windup and delivery. The ball will curve to the right of the plate. If you're throwing left-handed, remember to reverse the hold—the ball will curve to the left of the plate.

Hall of Famer Cy Young is baseball's all-time pitching legend. During his twenty-two-year career, Young won 511 games and lost only 316, a record that is almost 100 wins more than his nearest competitor. In addition, Young won twenty or more games per season for nine consecutive years.

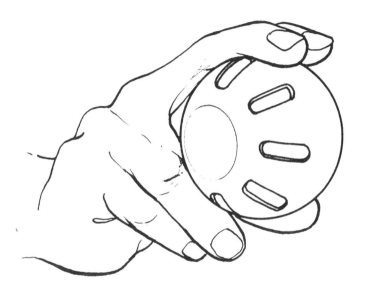

Carl Hubbell, who compiled a 253–154 win-loss record during his sixteen seasons, realized a pitcher's dream in the 1934 All-Star Game. On July 10, Hubbell, needing only twelve pitches, struck out future Hall of Famers Babe Ruth, Lou Gehrig, and Jimmie Foxx, with two men on base. At the start of the next inning, Hubbell struck out Al Simmons and Joe Cronin, for a total of five in a row!

The Slider

Another variation of the curveball is the slider. This is a pitch that looks like a fastball but moves slightly once it gets near the plate. You can use this one to fool batters; with the ball's speed, they'll think you've just thrown a fastball. As the ball approaches the plate, it will shift downward, just enough to cause the batter to swing over it.

To throw a slider, hold the ball between your thumb and your first and second fingers, with the slots facing forward. Compare your grip with the illustration to be certain you're holding the ball correctly. The grip for left-handed pitchers is the same. Use a standard windup to throw the slider.

There has been only one time in the history of major league baseball that a pitcher has thrown two consecutive no-hitters. Cincinnati pitcher Johnny Vander Meer shut down the Boston Braves on June 11, 1938. Four days later, he followed it up with a no-hit victory against the Brooklyn Dodgers.

Ron "Louisiana Lightning" Guidry, who pitched for the New York Yankees from 1975 to 1988, was one of the masters of the slider. His wickedly fast, ever-so-slightly breaking pitch bewildered and intimidated enough batters to give him a 1978 win-loss record of 25-3!

The Knuckleball

The knuckleball is baseball's weirdest pitch. A knuckleball bobs wildly as it approaches the plate, confusing the batter. Although not many pitchers can throw a knuckleball with a regular baseball, you'll be able to throw one with your Wiffle® ball that will probably have more movement than a pro's pitch!

To throw a knuckleball, grasp the Wiffle® ball along the seam with your fingers, with the fingernails of your first, second, and third fingers holding on to the ball. The slots in the ball should be facing directly forward. When pitching the ball, use a regular windup, but don't flick your wrist at the end of your delivery—push the ball away instead. The ideal knuckleball should rotate only one-half of a turn before it reaches the plate. That's not much when you consider that an average pitch spins sixteen times before reaching the plate.

Your knuckleballs will be slower than your other pitches, but that is the nature of the pitch. A slow knuckleball, if well thrown, will confuse even the best hitter.

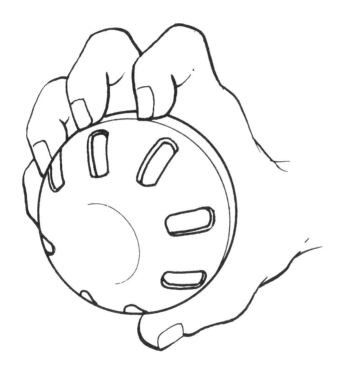

One of the masters of the knuckleball was the legendary Phil Niekro, who won 318 games during his twenty-four-year pitching career. Niekro, like many other pitchers who rely on the fluttering pitch, can't explain why it flies so crazily.

The Change-up

One particularly useful pitch is the change-up. This is a pitch that fools the batter into thinking that you are throwing a fastball—but instead, the ball approaches the plate relatively slowly. It is important not to let batters see how you're holding the ball for this pitch, because you want them to think that you're throwing a fastball.

The key to throwing a change-up is in the grip. First form an "OK" symbol with your fingers by touching the tips of your thumb and first finger together, and place the ball in your hand. The slots should be facing your palm. Throw it like a regular fastball; the special grip will slow the ball as it leaves your hand. If you throw this pitch with a windup like the one you use for your fastball, you'll probably fool the batter right off the plate. This is a good pitch to throw sandwiched in between your other pitches, because batters aren't expecting the ball to come in so slowly and will take their swings early.

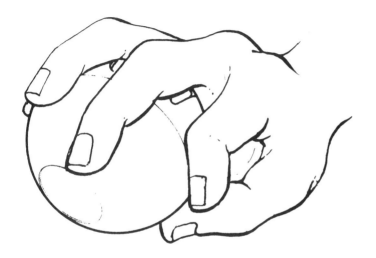

It only takes a fraction of a second for a batter's swing to be off enough to cause a foul ball. For example, when a 90-mph fastball is thrown, it reaches the plate in less than half a second. If a batter misjudges the arrival of the ball by as little as two thousandths of a second, a foul ball often results. Pitchers often use the change-up so that batters misjudge the speed of the pitch and strike out.

 Sinker

The sinker is a pitch that drops down right before it reaches home plate. To throw a sinker, hold the ball between your thumb and your first two fingers, with the slots facing away from your palm. Spread your first two fingers apart slightly, as in the illustration. Throw the ball with a standard pitching motion, releasing it with a slight flick of your wrist. The pitch should fly like a fastball, but slow down and drop slightly as it approaches the plate.

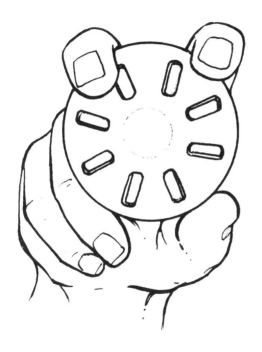

The record holder for no-hitters is Nolan Ryan, who pitched an incredible seven of them! This record easily surpasses the accomplishment of the pitcher with the most overall wins, Cy Young, who had a still remarkable three in his career. Ryan came close to getting even more no-hitters, hurling twelve one-hitters.

Riser

A riser—or rising fastball—is a pitch that sinks a little in the middle of its approach to the plate but then, as it gets closer to the plate, starts to climb. This is a hard pitch to hit, but it's also a challenging one to learn to throw.

To throw the riser, hold the ball between your thumb and your first and second fingers, with the slots facing your palm. Instead of throwing with a straight overhead windup, let your arm swing out to the side a little as you go through your pitching motion. With practice, you will be able to throw a pitch that will climb as it reaches the plate.

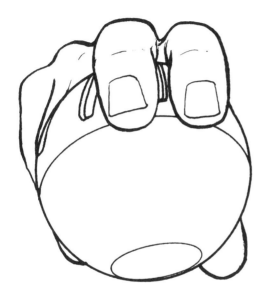

Leroy "Satchel" Paige was one of the best pitchers ever to play the game. During a single exhibition game, Paige struck out legends Charlie Gehringer and Jimmie Foxx three times each, and the great Rogers Hornsby five times!

Pitching Tips

Remember to not let batters see your pitching hand as you wind up—you want them to keep guessing what kind of pitch you're throwing, until it's too late. The key to pitching like a pro is just that—keep the batter guessing and you'll always have the advantage. For example, you might start out with a low fastball for the first couple of pitches. The batter will then be expecting a fastball, and when you throw a change-up or a curveball, chances are his or her timing will be off enough to get a strike. Using different pitches, and developing a strategy when you pitch, is crucial to becoming a good pitcher.

A helpful hint for making it easier to throw breaking pitches with your Wiffle® ball is to scuff up the side of the ball that doesn't have the slots. You can do this by rubbing the ball with some sandpaper or simply by rubbing the ball on some rough cement, such as a sidewalk. If the ball is roughed up a bit, your pitches will curve more dramatically. But don't try this with a real baseball—it's against the rules.

When a pitcher throws a game in which nobody so much as reaches first base, it's called a perfect game. A perfect game is the dream of all pitchers. In the big leagues, there have been only fifteen perfect games ever pitched. Perhaps the greatest one occurred in the 1956 World Series, when New York Yankees pitcher Don Larsen hurled a perfect game against the Brooklyn Dodgers. The most recent perfect game was pitched by Dennis Martinez, then with the Montreal Expos, in a 1991 game against the Los Angeles Dodgers. Other pitchers who have thrown perfect games include Catfish Hunter, Sandy Koufax, and Jim Bunning.

Home Run Derby

In this game, one player pitches while the others hit. The object of the game is to "score" home runs. In addition to hitting the ball into the home run zone, home runs can be scored by getting five hits. A hit is any ball knocked in fair territory that is not caught in the air by a fielder. A fielded grounder counts as a hit. Four balls equals a walk, which counts as a hit. The number of outs per inning can be determined by the players before the game, but for this game one out seems to work best. A player remains at bat until three strikes are thrown without a hit, or a fly ball or line drive is caught. At this time, the player who just made the out becomes the pitcher.

Every time the batter gets either five hits or a home run, a point is scored. For example, if a batter has five hits and three home runs and then makes an out, he or she finishes the inning with a total of four points. If a player has a number of hits that don't add up to a home run and then makes an out, the hits are lost.

Play rotates until everyone has batted. At that point the inning is over. Any number can play, and if there are more than two, the others serve as outfielders, attempting to catch fly balls. Players should decide the length of the game, based on reaching a set number of points or innings.

Setting Boundaries

A fenced-in backyard works best as a playing field, because you can use the fence to denote the home run area. If a fenced-in area is not available, choose an open spot and pick a boundary that will serve as the home run area. Any ball hit past the boundary will count as a home run. Also, pick two points that will serve as foul-ball boundaries. Trees or other large objects work well. If no natural markers exist, use pine cones or any other object to serve as markers for the foul lines. In addition, pick a spot for home plate. A spot near a wall or fence is best so that a strike zone can be created. An area on a wall or fence can be used as the strike zone to determine balls and strikes.

Any ball that hits the designated area is a strike, and any ball that hits outside that area is a ball. If no wall or fence exists and there are more than two players, the third player can serve as catcher *and* umpire. The umpire determines balls and strikes in this case. Once all of the boundaries are determined, set an area for the pitching mound and begin play.

Be creative and make up your own games. It doesn't take much space to play baseball with the Wiffle® ball, and you need only one or two other players to get a game going. By practicing your pitches with a batter, you'll know what works and what doesn't. With practice, you'll be able to take what you've learned here and develop your own special strike-out pitch.

> Play ball!